MISSION
IMPOSSIBLE

MISSION
IMPOSSIBLE

PROJECT MANAGEMENT TIPS TO IMPLEMENT DIGITAL PROJECTS SUCCESSFULLY

G. MEGAVARNAN

Notion Press

Old No. 38, New No. 6
McNichols Road, Chetpet
Chennai - 600 031

First Published by Notion Press 2017
Copyright © G. Megavarnan 2017
All Rights Reserved.

ISBN 978-1-946822-31-4

DISCLAIMER

This book is weaved around a true story but all characters are fictional. The opinions and concepts are not necessarily based on the experience around the story timeline but based on the overall life experiences of the author. Any resemblance to actual persons, living or dead, or actual events is purely coincidental.

DEDICATION

To my father Late. Mr. P. Govindaswamy and
my mother R. Muniyammal who had provided me
the best education inspite of all the odds and difficulties.

To my wife Kanchana Devi who always encouraged me
to pursue my professional passions.

To my mentors Mr. Govind and Mr. Sriram.

CONTENTS

THE REASON BEHIND
THIS BOOK

As an young entrepreneur, one of my goal was to be a published author. I always looked up to people who have written books. Though there has been many books in the current topic I always felt that management is an art and same rules doesn't suit all. Hence felt that I should write something that would give the audience a feel that would potentially suit their situation too, like an astrologer guiding the customer with "guideline" solutions which the customer can fit in appropriately to suit his/her need.

The purpose of this book is to help implement your digital projects successfully. When you did apply any of these techniques for your situation please drop me a note at gmegavarnan@gmail.com. I would love to hear that.

Good Luck

G. Megavarnan

ACKNOWLEDGEMENTS

I want to thank the following people who have played an important part in getting this book out.

1. My lovely two daughters Miss. Kansateshri and Miss. Akshara who always teased me from writing.

2. My close friends Mr. Kumaran and Mr. Bala who always encouraged me to succeed in all my new endeavours.

3. The Indus Enterprenuer Organization and Mr. Praveen Sekhar & Mrs. Akhila of TIE who sparked me to write this book

4. Mr. Kirubha Shankar who made book writing so simple and built the confidence that I can become an author some day.

5. The wonderful team at NotionPress including Nirmal Pradeep, Ann and Mr. Naveen for their excellent support.

6. Miss. Aishwarya for helping me type the whole book patiently.

7. All the participants of the annual "Book Authoring retreats."

GETTING STARTED

Congratulations on starting to read this book. The very fact that you are even reading this book means that you have given your digital project's success a serious thought.

I always believe that every problem is unique and every solution is unique like every human being unique. Having said this, please read this book as a sequence of events that got enacted in a project drama and try and understand in what situation I have applied these techniques and how.

I also believe that management is an art and all of us learn to manage from the day we are born into this world.

Happy learning...

1

THE BURNING DESIRE

Clean roads, cars and buses plying at significant speed, people walking on the pedestrian listening to music...good food...lots of shopping, people speaking in tamil all around...what more do you need...wow!!! After having a stupendous lunch at KomalaVillas restaurant on a Sunday and standing on the main road near City Hall metro station in Singapore, it felt so nice. I was wondering how successful I had been in the last three years and I was praising God for all that he had given to me so far. But still...something was missing. I didn't quite know what it was exactly...Family? Friends? Relatives? Culture? I wasn't sure. The urge to return back to India was suddenly going up and at that second I met Ravi, who informed me about the recruitment happening in Singapore for a leading IT company based in Chennai. I felt I should definitely try this and should not miss it at any cost.

Next day morning, I managed to fix an appointment for an interview in the evening. It was around 4PM and I was all excited to discuss about my job (more than the job, my future and the inner desire to go back to India was kicking in me). My turn came and there I met Mr. Adi K, the C. E. O of the company. In two hours, I was fully convinced that this was the company that would take me to heights and allow me to grow in Chennai. Within a few hours, I received the offer letter directly from the company and took the most serious, bold and happy decision to return back to India and renounce my Singapore permanent resident status too. Most of my friends were against my decision. In fact, even I felt that God had been very kind to me all these years and I could probably be among the very few who had got the Singapore PR for self and family at a very early age. But still my heart decided I should go back home and the important reason was the comfort and commitment that Mr. Adi K gave as well as the details about his company and the work they do.

4th Jan 2001

I joined the IT Company in Chennai with a lot of dreams and aspirations. Immediately I was assigned as a tech lead for a U. S based project. We were a team of four people and it was a Java project. I had very good team members and an excellent project manager too. Though it was a tough assignment, we somehow managed to do it on time. As a tech lead, I travelled to the U. S for implementation. After the successful completion of my job, I returned to a lot of appreciation from the customer, management and my team.

By then (within six months), my probation period was over and I was confirmed and also promoted to the role of a Project Leader. This time I was given a bigger team and bigger responsibilities. With a lot of excitement I started working in the new project and things were going quite well. After a couple of months a new project manager, Varun, joined the project and started finding faults with everything and everyone including myself. I was slowly getting frustrated and as days passed by he became more and more irritating. Couple of weeks from then Varun decided unilaterally that I am a non performer and sent a note to HR to sack me from the company. The HR manager called me to a room and asked me to resign and leave immediately.

I didn't know who said "Heavens Won't Fall" but I definitely felt "Hell Will Fall" as long as managers like Varun live in this world. My mind was racing without knowing how to handle this situation and I excused myself from the HR manager and slipped out. Trusting Mr. Adi's rosy words I returned back to India but now in less than ten months the draconian Varun decided unilaterally that I am a non performer and sent me out of my job. Soon I realized that along with me, a couple of other project managers were also asked to leave in the same fashion. I also understood that the reason for actual retrenchment could be that I was highly paid for that role. But still what I couldn't digest was the fact that Varun called me a non performer. This very statement hurt me a lot and I was finding it difficult to recoup from it.

Not knowing what to do, on my way back home, I stopped my green color Maruthi car near the tea shop opposite Anna Library. I was just cursing my fate and myself for deciding to come back to India. Right now, all I could think of was how I could become a performer again. Both my wife and parents were very supportive. But my mind was wandering all over. In the midst of heavy traffic near the signal, the continuous honking of the horns, and my own mind racing madly, I heard my phone ringing faintly. Unwillingly I picked up my phone but didn't bother to say "hello" and open up the conversation. However, from the other end I heard this girl who asked me, "Sir, we are looking for someone like you and would you be interested for a solution architect role in Computer Services Company". Oh!! What a timing, and I said absolutely. She continued and finally checked if I can take the interview in the next two hours. I was perplexed but I accepted and immediately drove down to Tidel Park.

After completing the security checks I went to the third floor and sat in the reception. Just in front of me I saw a customer testimony hanging carrying an appreciation for the good work in a particular project. I felt that I should not only clear the interview and take a job but went a step ahead and decided that a similar customer testimony should hang on the same wall with my name in it.

To my surprise, I not only cleared the interview but also received an offer letter with 20% jump from the current salary the same day. I felt like jumping up and down and was on cloud nine. The HR asked me to join ASAP. Even though I was very happy, the one and only thought that I had was to prove to Varun that I am not a nonperformer.

10th Dec 2001 – 9:15AM

I was in the reception and was asked to wait for HR to complete the initial formalities. I kept looking at the customer testimony intently. With a confused look the receptionist asked me "Sir, that is a customer testimony given for the good work we do. But, why are you looking at it so intently?" Without turning but nodding my head I said, "Soon my customer testimony will hang here". The receptionist was slightly taken aback but appreciated and wished me good luck. The HR came and escorted me and the receptionist raised her thumb towards the testimony with a warm smile. I felt like 1000 butterflies were flying inside me. The feeling was similar to that when you get when you see your first love... oh!!! What a feeling!! But at the same time, the draconian, Varun's face crossed by and sucked the very moment and further moments to come.

"In this book I have uncovered how the burning desire has made me creative enough to turn around a deep red project successfully.

The burning desire of Mr. Lee Kuan Yew transformed Singapore from a tiny poor island to a wealthiest country in Asia in 3 decades.

When you desire something the whole universe conspires to help you make it happen – Quote from Paulo Coelho."

2

TRUST YOURSELF

Few days passed by and I was getting familiar with the people and processes. While I was happy, every now and then the draconian, Varun kept crossing my mind in a zig-zag pattern which actually pulled me deep down. It was getting hard for me to come out of the Varun phenomenon and I slowly started feeling that my mind was getting rusted with negativity which was only counterproductive. On Friday, morning after beating all the security measures I stepped into the ground floor of Tidel Park. As usual I was frisked by the security team and after a couple of minutes I bumped into Rajiv, a good friend of mine, who had come to Tide for an interview. He was one another person who was affected by Varun. He was quite happy to see that I had gotten a job and couldn't understand why my face was still pale and unhappy. And I started explaining how I was sucked by Varun's thoughts even though I got a nice job. For a few moments both of us remained silent and he bluntly told "remove your sucking thoughts and add trust in yourself." Though it sounds simple, I felt "trusting ourselves" was the key. He went on to say that "Thalaiva, if you can get a job in a day with 20% hike while you are jobless, it means a lot and first understand that. Someone has put in their faith in you and believes that you have great calibre. Please do not disappoint them and yourself too." He continued and started mentioning that all of them who got sacked along with me are still looking for jobs and I am still whining. I felt very bad for the others and felt quite completely relieved from the Varun pain after listening to his positive conversation.

Next day morning with a positive attitude, a burning desire and self-trust, I stepped into the office. Nancy (receptionist) gave a big smile and raised "Thumbs-up". I paused for a while in front of her and said thank you. Nancy continued and said "Sir, I was indeed thrilled when you were saying that your testimony should be hanging here in a year's time. So how is that journey going sir?" I paused for a moment and said, "It is just starting". With my head held high and a burning desire and self-trust, I accessed into the Curie hall. I'd just taken a few steps when my resource head, Mr. SKV took me to the corner and allocated me a cubicle. With happiness and a smile, I was pleased with the allocated seat and bidding good bye to Mr. SKV, I was looking at my cubicle and the surrounding places.

It was a nice cosy corner cubicle. In front of my cubicle the company's Directors were seated and to my left, a fresh set of minds from India's top-B schools were seated and parallel to my cubicle there was a small team of 3–4 people huddling together and arguing on some subject. There were a few cubicles behind me too. I soon realized that the cubicle seat is a privileged seat and only managers and their seniors were allocated those seats. I remembered yesterday's conversation with my friend Rajiv and felt that I am blessed to have gotten this better break. May be God had decided that I should be successful. Who knows may be I wouldn't be what I am today, writing a book if I had not been sacked fifteen years ago. God is great. While I was still in my own world of thoughts, Mr. SKV patted me and took me back to the delivery head, Mr. Pillai. Mr. Pillai was the one who had recruited me. Mr. Pillai started moving with a tone of familiarity and assigned me into the Expoworld project as the Solution Architect. I was quite thrilled to get into a technical role but frankly I was equally nervous. Someone knocked at the transparent glass door and came inside Mr. Pillai's cabin. Mr. Pillai then introduced him as Mr. Dharani and his role as the project leader for the Expoworld project. Quickly I could recognize that he was part of that small team which was involved in the heated arguments a while ago. Mr. Dharni was cold and unwilling to shake hands. Probably observing this, after Mr. Dharani left the room, both Mr. SKV and Mr. Pillai advised me to focus on solution architecture and not to get involved in the day-to-day project management activities. Hiding my discomfort, I exchanged thank you notes and went back to my cubicle and sat quietly. After a short while Mr. Dharani walked up to my cubicle and started having friendly chats and both of us went out for coffee. Soon both me and Dharani shared a warm relationship and both of us realized we play independent roles. I could sense a sigh of relief from Mr. Dharani's face. After going back to our seats, Mr. Dharani exchanged important project related documents. A lot of them in fact. I was actually overwhelmed after glancing at them quickly. Post lunch I was fully engrossed into the project and slowly started realizing that it was the best assignment that I could possibly get. Again I felt God is great and indeed started thanking Varun for sacking me and started trusting myself to make this a big success.

"self trust is the first secret of success

– Ralph Waldo Emerson"

3

REEL-TO-REAL

20th Dec 2001

Around 8:00AM, the whole of Tidel Park was glittering with Christmas lights. The two wheelers and four wheelers car parking were kind of getting empty with all the night shift employees going/gone back to their homes. A group of young men and girls were sipping their morning coffee and some along with cigarettes. Security guys were rushing to get their things right while the crowd was still less. Noticing all this I was waiting for the lift and next to me was a retired senior officer of the Tide building. I have seen him few times before and after initial introductions we shook hands and got out of the lift. I walked past the reception area and gazed at the testimony. I was smiling inside and felt that somewhere deep in my heart the thought of hanging my testimony in the reception area had sunk in. Though I had done architectural work in my earlier projects, this seemed to be quite big and also the expectations from the customer were quite different than my earlier experiences. Around 11:45AM, Mr. SKV brought along with him a thin / slim and tall guy wearing thick glasses and introduced him as Chandran and as the go-to-guy for all business requirements. Oh!! That was really a moment of relief to see a business guy as I was really consumed by the huge set of requirements for over a week. After initial introductions Mr. SKV left and Chandran took me for coffee.

Chandran is a coffee lover which I realized later. I also learnt later that he takes people to coffee shops to generally discuss "problems"☺. In fact the team used to tease me that I dug myself into the problem even after warnings from Chandran. The coffee vendor seemed to have changed and set up the shop newly today and Chandran was reluctant to buy coffee from the new vendor. I quickly realized that Chandran was very particular about the details. In fact, this trait of his had come handy many times during our meetings with customers. But to Chandran's surprise the coffee was very good and both of us had our rounds of introduction. It was interesting for me to realize how Chandran had transformed himself into a businessman after graduating from a computer science engineering college. Chandran was young, energetic, with loads of knowledge on the subject. During my conversations, I started realizing that I was into an excellent assignment where I could learn phenomenal knowledge on the most interesting and growing field in IT digital management.

After a brief introduction on the technology concepts and customer requirements, both of us went back to our seats. Again for an hour I started reading from the beginning and felt very easy to relate to what the customer wanted. With a sigh of relief, I thought I should go for lunch and came out of my cubicle and started walking. A young, well-dressed guy came out of the lane and with a very firm handshake introduced himself as AK and joined me for lunch. After a brief conversation, both of us realized that we are in the same project and I quickly realized that unlike Chandran, AK is completely technical. AK was very thorough on Java/J2EE, web servers, application servers and especially the IBM stack and he had a technical mastery in his subject.

Post lunch I felt that the customer requirement was getting easier to understand. The name of the Project was Expoworld and it was aimed to create an online trade fair experience and aimed to become the largest / biggest online trade fair platform for the whole of Italy.

A staggering 10 million+ Italian citizens were expected to register into this platform and through this platform, the customer expected the below features broadly,

    a.   Search for the products that they are looking to buy

    b.   Identify the booth that sells this product

    c.   Should be able to see the product details

d. Once they like the products they should be able to buy directly or through an auction mechanism.

e. Visitors' management including their profiling, loyalty building, various classifications etc.

The critical factors to consider were

- 10 million+registrants totally

- 10000+online visitors /day

- 1000+Users at the same time

- 100 mb size of data and product.

- 10000+product catalogue

- 1000+online booths

- 1000+auctions/day

- 1 million financial transactional/day.

Absolutely mind blowing. Especially fifteen years ago when online/e-commerce was just kicking. I felt that architecting a solution of this magnitude was definitely a daunting task. Imagining the solution is much easier but making it work is not easy at all. Realizing this I started focusing on the non-functional requirements of the application. The most critical requirements were 99. 99 % uptime, environment stability and scalability.

BUILD vs. BUY

The very first strategic decision that had to be taken was whether the customer would like to build from scratch or buy COTS products and tailor them to their needs.

I made the customer lean towards BUY. Taking a conscious decision at the start of the engagement on this was quite supportive and provided the much needed clarity on the architectural aspects.

ENVIRONMENT and INTERGRATION CO-EXIST

The customer and I realized that just one product is not going to provide them all the features and definitely multiple products would be required for the overall solution. Now the next question that had to be addressed was the products that should be working on the "Environment Layer". So this lead us to the important task of choosing the right environment. We chose IBM websphere as the defacto platform. The core reason for us to make that decision was the compatibility that all the products (portal, search, auction, etc.) had.

SERVER SIZING

The next important point was what kind of server configuration had to be considered based on the non-functional specifications. Like EMI calculators, the servers can also be sized and determined. What we did as part of the sizing was only theoretical in nature. However, to make the solution perfect, we decided to engage the IBM hardware team professionally. As part of the hardware purchase deal, we structured to get the sizing evaluated in their simulation environment. In fact, to be on the safer side, 20% increase to the server configuration parameters were made and this indeed helped when after a year of going live, at times the traffic during trade fair days were heavily high. During these times, increased server configuration did come handy. This point may not be of great value these days considering the huge technology improvements. However, fundamentally it would be prudent to do the server sizing taking into consideration your non-functional requirements like usage, load etc.

LOGICAL ARCHITECTURE

Post completion of the environmental architecture, it was important for me to put together a logical architecture that would depict how the various functional features would be delivered and through which product they would be delivered. This particularly was a daunting task as one needed to have the complete picture and idea about the project in its entirety. Chandran was very supportive during this period. Along with Chandran, Kasinath was also very helpful. I will introduce Kasinath to you at a later stage.

To recap on major functional requirements

- User profiling
- Product catalogue
- Booth management
- Search
- Auction
- Visitor management

The important aspect was to choose products that would integrate and co-exist among each other. The list of products considered were

- Portal product
- Search product
- Auction engine
- ERP that would maintain the product catalogues pricing and payment.

Multiple or many rounds of discussions with various vendors, understanding their earlier case studies, their architecture coverage on NFS, fitting environment, integration with one another had to be checked and understood. This was a daunting task as every vendor would try to sell all rosy features. What was crucial was whether these products would co-exist and work seamlessly. Similar to good individuals turning bad when asked to work together in a team, good products will turn out to be bad when integrated. During this phase, AK was very supportive. AK and self-use to read volumes of product documentation to understand the product fine prints.

POC (Proof of Concept)

Once the logical architecture was in place, the key thing that the customer and I decided was to actually check if all of these products would really work together seamlessly. With the help of Mr. Dharani and his team, we did small POC's and checked the integration part. For all practical purposes, in the given time, we managed to just satisfy ourselves but couldn't do an elaborate integration. On the contrary, if we keep doing POC's to prove every point, we may or may not have enough time to deliver the project too. So, this is a fine grey line and many a times hunch matters and self-trust helps.

4

A NEW AVATAR

Mar 2002

I was working almost independently and directly with the customers over the last two months. It was quite a time consuming responsibility and never really got into the team's day-to-day tasks except for the interactions that used to happen for the technical knowhow and POC's.

During these interactions I use to feel that the skill level of the team was relatively low and the teams were struggling. However, since my role was solution architect and also due to the initial warning from Mr. Pillai I seldom tried to understand the details.

At the same time, slowly and steadily, the customer's confidence on the architecture and solution increased. However, the customer's confidence on the project team was slowly coming down and the customer started complaining. Every now and then Chandran, AK and others use to crib about this problem. But beyond that nothing happened. Mr. Dharani, I am sure was aware too but wasn't sure as why he wouldn't take any corrective actions. I have always felt that Mr. Dharani would just be keen to know the status and update that in the excel sheets. For example, he would only be interested in updating whether the task got completed or whether it was pending. If it was pending beyond updating in excel, he wouldn't bother to go deeper and understand the problem and try and fix it. May be he saw a limitation in the role. May be he thought that was the technical leader's role and he being a project leader doesn't have to go deep into the problem. Or maybe he thought his role was only to provide the status to the management and other stake holders. I never understood his approach until the end of the engagement. In fact, he is doing well for himself. Even now when I think about him, I really can't gauge which is right and which is wrong. Maybe he was right and he was just doing what he was supposed to do as he assumed his role to be. I will probably leave it at this.

4th Mar 2002 – 8:30AM

I normally come on time to the office and most often than not, I would be the only the person sitting in the corner cubicle early. Along with me, my super boss, Mr. Krishnan, would come in early. In fact he would be a bit earlier to the office many times. Mr. Krishnan looks simple and humble. Educated from India's premier institutes, he was the head of the unit and was couple of levels away to the CEO of the company. Normally Mr. Krishnan would be undisturbed, cool and calm and would handle all problems effortlessly. However for some reason he looked quite disturbed that day and while passing by my cubicle to his corner office he signaled me to come into his office.

I was talking / meeting him for the first time. I have seen only a very few people interacting / meeting him. Everyone had given a few frightening views about him and I was a bit scared as I didn't know the possible reason for his meeting request. I was trying to take all possible project related details from the architecture side. I was remembering the nice comments that the customer was sharing about the architecture work to both Chandran and me. In fact I could feel my heart beat rising and I started sweating a bit. I hadn't felt like this in the last five years of my professional career. My mind started recollecting the various views that the colleagues had about him. For example "no one can easily answer him and he will cross the question in various ways which would put you in greater difficulty" and "he will never smile or give a comforting look while talking".

Slowly I walked near Mr. Krishnan's room. I have observed that all cabins are closed with doors but with a small see through glass. Looking through the glass I knocked at the door. Mr. Krishnan just signaled me to come inside. I was pleasantly surprised to see Mr. Krishnan warmly welcome me and asking about me, my family etc. Slowly he started asking about my experience, the technologies I worked with, my capabilities etc. It was almost like an interview but in a very nice manner and finally he asked me to leave. I just couldn't understand much. I quietly left the room and came back to my cubicle and sat there. I kind of felt a filter coffee would help. Recently corporate services introduced a fresh filter coffee vendor so that associates need not to go a long way for coffee. In fact many of the no project acquaintances happened there in the coffee shop for me. Yes, that day I met the Finance Executive Mr. Ratnam. Mr. Ratnam was one of the senior most employees. He was very friendly and started talking about his initial days in Kaka towers. In fact this unit was an independent consulting unit which was then acquired by my company. Then I slowly understood that though the company was big in size the delivery experiences at a unit level were limited and I started to kind of understand why Mr. Krishnan was trying to find out more on my project implementation and quality process experiences. Mr. Ratnam was very strong on shares and started talking about those topics. After almost half an hour of discussions both of us realized that we had spent too much time and slowly people started coming and the clock was ticking ten plus.

Both Mr. Ratnam and I started walking back to our cubicles. In not more than ten minutes the office attendant came to my cubicle and told that my boss Mr. Pillai had called me to his office. Mr. Pillai regularly invites me for project discussions and would give me lot of technical inputs. I thought I am being called for the same reason and started walking back casually without being aware of the forthcoming news. Without much hesitation I just knocked at the glass door (this set of rooms had transparent glass doors) and entered the room with a smile. I always used to wonder why some rooms were left transparent and some were closed. May be they were designed with a purpose so that hierarchy is maintained. I never got the right reason though. To my shock, when I looked inside through the transparent door I could sense that Mr. Pillai was little unwelcoming and he started shooting lots of process related questions. I was little perplexed and was unsure how I should handle the questions. In my first job I was put in quality department for three full months and was also promoted as a quality lead for a short while. Since I was also involved in the quality certification process, I was completely familiar with all the SDLC processes and in no matter of time Mr. Pillai was impressed indeed. Mr. Pillai bluntly asked me whether I will be able to perform the project manager role. Colleagues have advised me earlier about how Mr. Pillai is straight and strict and how one should answer in tough times. Those advices came really handy and I told Mr. Pillai that I would be able to perform the role but that I need little time to ascertain. Mr. Pillai advised me how the new role would be of help to me to grow within the organization etc. In an hour's time Mr. Pillai walked past my cubicle and asked me "Ennappa-what have you decided?" Without hesitation I gave the standard reply, like everyone else, "Ok sir" without realizing what I am getting into for the next one year or so. With a smile on his face, Mr. Pillai entered into Mr. Krishnan's room and in five minutes, I got an email that said I will be the PM henceforth. I was really stunned at the quick decisions. Yeah, over the next nine months I was actually pushed to take these kinds of decisions and I staunchly believe that this experience is what has made me what I am today. Quick, bold, simple and strategic decisions. Yeah in the coming chapters I am trying to uncover these practical situations and my experiences.

5

THE BIG PICTURE

The next morning I had a conference call with Mr. Ramesh, project director, who operates out of Delhi. After all the initial welcoming talks he started sharing the real status. He was repeatedly insisting that the project is in DEEP RED status and the possible reason why he says so could be that 90% of the tasks aren't completed as on date. But beyond this, Mr. Ramesh couldn't articulate as to what could be the problem or solution etc. The only thing that evolved was I got scared in two hours seeing the project plan. Mr. Ramesh is a seasoned delivery person and he had a knack to understand the status. But somehow I felt that he hadn't got the real status. May be he was shown just the status "completed/pending" and maybe he was operating around that aspect. At around 11:00AM the conference call got over and I badly needed a coffee break!! Now, I felt that I should go down to the ground floor for coffee and not inside so that the break would be little longer. I was moving forward with the project status thoughts completely engrossing me. And I saw AK, Chandran, Raj, Lamech and Subbarayulu walking together.

I ordered coffee and some biscuits for all of us and had informal introduction with all of them. During the course of the chat I realized that the project is in DEEP RED. What caused me more worry was the fact that I was unable to understand the core reasons for the RED status. Except Chandran, the others weren't having an idea on the full project. AK was explaining about e-booth functionalities and Raj was talking about search functionalities but more or less in silos only. Chandran mentioned that I should talk to Dharani too and I was hoping that I would get some understanding on the core reasons when I speak to Dharani. I was looking for Dharani and realized that he was yet to come to office. Couple of hours later Dharani came to my cubicle and both of us went into the conference room. I was asking Dharani to give me a detailed overview of the project keeping the status in mind. After almost an hour I could barely understand only a few modules names and some random status like "in progress", "yet to be started", "completed" etc. these were the statuses of the tasks listed on excel. In fact there was a task mentioned on excel which had no relevance to the project as the customer changed the requirement but it was still reflecting as "in progress". Sighting this I asked who is doing this particular task and why is someone doing it. Dharani wasn't able to explain further. Soon I realized that the team hadn't understood the big picture. I requested Chandran to give a detailed project overview to the entire team touching upon.

- Objectives of the project −why?
- All the features of the project −what?
- All the various users −who? of the project and their access rights
- Revenue Model −how?

Along with Chandran, I prepared a couple of slides on the architecture. I had booked the calendar of the entire team for 11:00AM the next day for about two hours followed by lunch outing to a restaurant near Thiruvanmayuir. I also invited Mr. Pillai for the team lunch. While Mr. Pillai excused himself, he promptly approved the lunch from company budget.

Next day the entire team (around eight members, 1-project level, 1-BA, 5Developers, 1-PM /Architecture) assembled into the Newton conference room. Tea and snacks were organized. I welcomed the team and quickly requested Chandran to provide the team an overview of the project. Though I had a complete picture of the architecture and project, Chandran's explanation was excellent. End of the session I too got lots of clarifications. After Chandran completed his session I touched upon the technical (logical) architecture and how the technology is trying to deliver the business requirements. End of the session the entire team thanked for organizing the big picture workshop and that did really have made them understand (to some extent) the functionalities in full. With all smiles and satisfaction the entire team went out for lunch. During the course of the lunch I explained that every team member should have a clear idea of the overall project goal and vision of the project, their contribution in the project and how that contribution will affect/impact the common goal. The team kind of understood and I could see a sense of satisfaction in all their eyes. Chandran while returning stopped by and took my hand and told "Thank you Mega. Now I feel that we will deliver the project successfully at any cost". I could feel that Chandran said that genuinely and was in fact it was overwhelming and slowly I could see a sense of responsibility clicking into me. Not stopping here I told that this big picture will be conducted every fortnight for the next two months and that workshop will be delivered by the members themselves in turns.

This big picture / fortnight initiative by team members on rotation was later considered as the best practice and many projects started following it. The critical advantage, especially in "Digital Projects".

    a.   Every team member understands where his/her work is plugged into the overall project environment.

    b.   When changes are made to the code he/she gets to visualize the potential integration aspects.

    c.   The sense of ownership from the team members become quite high.

"One day a traveller, walking along a lane, came across 3 stonecutters working in a quarry. Each was busy cutting a block of stone. Interested to find out what they were working on, he asked the first stonecutter what he was doing. "I am cutting a stone!" Still no wiser the traveller turned to the second stonecutter and asked him what he was doing. "I am cutting this block of stone to make sure that it's square, and its dimensions are uniform, so that it will fit exactly in its place in a wall." A bit closer to finding out what the stonecutters were working on but still unclear, the traveller turned to the third stonecutter. He seemed to be the happiest of the three and when asked what he was doing replied: "I am building a cathedral.""

This story beautifully illustrates a key leadership quality – seeing the bigger picture. All three stonecutters were doing the same thing, but each gave a very different answer.

Each knew how to do his job but what was it that set the third stonecutter apart? Perhaps:

- *Knowing not just how and what to do, but knowing why.*

- *Viewing the whole and not just its parts.*

- *Seeing a vision, a sense of the bigger picture.*

- *Having the ability to see significance in work, beyond the obvious.*

- *Understanding that a legacy will live on, whether in the stone of a cathedral, or in the impact made on other people.*

6

THE PLAN

8th Mar 2002 – 6PM

That evening we had a customer status meeting. The status update meetings happen via conference calls. Mr. Galasso had joined for the status call and from our side Chandran, Dharani and I attended it. This was my first weekly status update meeting with the customer and I planned to be a listener and wanted Dharani to present the status as usual. Chandran started the call and requested Dharani to provide the status update. Dharani opened the excel sheet and started reading out the various tasks listed there and its level of completion. The customer had the status report but it was more like a monologue from Dharani and it went on for about ten minutes. Chandran was trying to bring his views and was providing his comments. I was witnessing this and felt a bit uncomfortable, though I wasn't sure why I felt so. What was even more unnerving was the fact that the customer was absolutely quite. The call went for about half an hour and kind of closed passively and all of us came out of the room. Normally in status calls customers grill and try to understand the current project situation threadbare but now in our case it was completely opposite. I took Chandran for a coffee break and expressed my feeling and Chandran did accept that he too felt the same. He went on to say that this type of meeting has been going on for long but I guess today the customer was very upset and maybe he was expecting me to share the status. The filter coffee arrived and after having a couple of sips Chandran told "Mega this filter / decoction seems to be home made." As he was saying I realized that this shop is new and the old guy had left. Out of curiosity, I asked what happened and the spontaneous reaction was "ozunga plan pannala athan moodittan" (Didn't plan properly hence he closed the shop). I was not sure as we have known the earlier shop guy but didn't feel like probing on it and left it as is. Moreover the coffee was good and hence didn't bother much. After a little while Chandran bumped into his old friend who is an Events Manager and during their conversation when Chandran was asking about the results of her latest event she reacted saying "Ozunga plan pannala adhan fail aaidchi". Chandran smiled and wished her luck for the upcoming project and both of us started walking back to our office. Inside the lift I met my old college friend Jai. Jai was a class topper and gold medallist. On seeing him I was pleasantly surprised and asked him "Hey enada inga irukka? (Hey what are you doing here?) You were going to the US for masters I thought". Jai reacted with a smile and told "No da I couldn't go and probably many reasons like money, bank collaterals, application timing, timely visa process etc. But simple a sollanumna ozunga plan pannala, athan US la poi padikkamudila." I was stunned not because of Jai's reply. But because of the fact that in all three instances the quoted reason for failure was "poor planning". This kind of hit me very hard in my mind. I started having some very deep thoughts and couldn't continue my work. I packed up my bags and returned home. While driving back, I was constantly thinking about the status update call, the unnerving silence during the entire status update call and failure vs. planning conversations from various cross-sections of people all at the same time. While I was deeply engaged in this thought, my phone started ringing and I quickly realized that the call is from Italy and it should be from the customer. I parked the car and attended the call. It was and with his thick accent he came straight to the point and told "Mega there is no clarity in today's update and you have to revisit the plan". I felt as if a big rock hit me hard on my head. went on to further discuss about his visit to India and in the end he thanked me for the solution architecture and conveyed that IBM had approved the architecture. Though I was elated at that remark I couldn't come out of the "Plan-Problem". What struck me hard was the coincidence of plan and failure. As I kept thinking about this I started scribbling the relationship between plan and failure and summarized it as

- "Planning is inversely proportional to Failure"
  - Higher the planning lower the Failure
  - Lower the planning higher the Failure
  - The farther and deeper the plan higher the success

Sounds simple and easy but then I felt that my immediate focus should be to plan. I was repeatedly thinking about this concept and the more I thought the stronger the thought became. With this thought, I reached home and as soon as I reached home my daughter and Devi (my wife) came out of the house and asked why I was so late and my reply was heavy traffic. May be since this was a standard dialogue she became upset and started saying "Ozunga plan pannina intha problem irukathu". My goodness, I was completely taken aback. Not knowing how to react, I stayed quite and moved on with dinner and other discussions. But this "Plan Vs. Failure" itch wasn't fading away from my thoughts.

Next day morning, with the itch continuing, I reached my office. By then Mr. Pillai had also reached the office and he called me to his cabin and showed me an email that had sent mentioning the lack of clarity, poor plan etc. kind of complain about Mr. Dharani. Though I was a little surprised by the approach, I agreed that I also felt the same. Mr. Pillai started explaining the importance of planning in personal life and also in projects, especially in Business Process Managements engagements.

In regular application development engagements the most important exercise at the start would be "Singing Off" the project scope. The very reason why this is done is to make sure the commercials doesn't get affected. Hence, the flow would be to

a. Gather all requirements

b. Scope them or boundary them

c. Write a detailed plan

d. Execute the plan

e. Don't Encourage changes as this affect time and effort

f. Charge for every change as change request

Whereas, in a typical Digital Management Engagements, the project execution flow would be as below,

- Understand the overall need

- Build a skeletal scope and don't boundary / wall them

- Break down the big project into small and manageable chunks

- Encourage change but manage it. Reason being both "business" and "process" needs to be "managed" and "management" is possible only when "change" is encouraged.

I was little confused but going back to the original "plan" problem, Mr. Pillai told me to make a larger plan covering the full project spectrum and also make detailed plans on every small chunk. It kind of made sense and he further advised that the larger plan should focus on timeline, constraints and dependencies and detailed plan should focus on all possible and required tasks (8–16 hours), owners of tasks, status tracking and detailed comments on task completion. Like for example, if someone is unable to do a particular task or if they are stuck or waiting for other tasks to complete then all of these should be commented and recorded and not just update the % completion and leave it at it. After a good solid discussion I started feeling the plan itch slowly receding in me.

7

MR. GALASSO-INDIA VISIT

24th Mar 2002 – 9:00AM

It was a nice Sunday morning around 9:00AM. Devi, my wife, had made the Sunday special idly and karikuzhambu (Mutton Gravy). After eating more than the required number of idlis (at times the taste bud overtakes your brain friends) I was feeling sleepy. But the thought that Mr.Galasso is arriving in Chennai from Italy was overwhelming and I was a bit excited too. The regular Mahabarath serial was being relayed in Vijay TV and Sun TV was airing the Solomon Pappaiya pattimandram. Slowly I got engrossed in Solomon and Raja's, Bharathi Baskar's witty comments until the phone started ringing. It was Chandran on the other side checking on the airport plans. I quickly changed over and started driving in my green Maruthi 800. SPB / Ilayaraja music was playing in my radio and though I am not a fan of music, sometimes I deeply engage in listening to music. Airport was just ten minutes from my home and since my dad was working at the airport, I had made some special arrangements for Chandran and myself to stand inside the airport and not wait outside. Soon Chandran joined me and both of us went inside the building. We saw the TV displaying the itineraries and realized we came a bit early. I think I have mentioned earlier too, Chandran is a filter coffee guy and he did quickly spot the coffee shop inside. After having idly I felt coffee is a nice idea and both of us ordered two filter coffees. Soon there was the announcement about the arrival of Mr. Galasso's flight and to our surprise we could spot him coming out earlier than expected.

After initial greetings, we took him to the hotel in a nice taxi. Our company had organized this quite well. I had asked my driver to bring the car along and all three of us went by taxi. It was a good half an hour's journey and Chandran explained Chennai, coffee, roads, cricket, movies, teams etc. Yes you guessed it right!! Both Mr. Galasso and I were just listening. Chandran is a good communicator and probably that is why he changed his track to business analyst role after doing his computer science engineering. After dropping him at the hotel, both of us returned back. It was a good ice breaker for myself and we had some good lighter moments. One of the core reasons for Mr. Galasso's trip to India was to visually / physically see the project's progress and also see the progress of the technical initiative which I had mentioned in the "REEL-to-REAL" chapter. Post that decision Mr. Dharani had formed a team that would be involved in the technical POC which included the following,

Feature	Product	Member Name
Search	Autonomy	Raj/Lamech
e-Booth	Epicentric	AK/Subbarayulu
Product Catalogue/Pricing	MFG Pro	Arvind
Auction	SIF	Subbarayulu
Visitor Management	Epicentric	AK

As a solution architect, I was Involved at a product level but not at the actual integration and coding and kind of handed over the actual implementation to delivery team lead by Dharani. If you remember I had mentioned earlier that the architecture and delivery was run independently. Though it helped in not getting influenced or biased by the delivery team, even today I feel that was the wrong decision. The delivery team, though capable in general and experienced in Java technology, what was required was the knowledge and know how on the technologies / product that are used in the project. Mr. Dharani failed to understand or probably he ignored the fact and instead was pushing the team to self – learn and deliver excellent results or maybe he possibly highlighted to management and since it would involve additional cost the management avoided it. All I felt was it is incorrect to push the team to learn everything by themselves and on top of it deploy them on live engagement and expect them to deliver projects on time and quality.

I certainly knew the POC hasn't come out well and the core idea for Mr. Galasso's two days trip to India was to check on the POC. As a project manager, I felt I should know how to handle the situation and not buckle down. Chandran and I were fully aware of the POC situation and did have a plan to manage this situation. In fact I would say that Mr. Chandran is quite capable in managing customer situations. What both of us were trying to do was quite risky but felt we didn't have much of a choice. Yes we decided we will start the presentation saying that the POC isn't working rather than trying to build useless stories and reasons. However, post confessing that the POC isn't working, we decided we will do the product demos. Chandran had also prepared power point slides on how the functionality will be technically delivered using the products. On top of it we had also prepared a detailed risk–mitigation plan.

Chandran and I presented our whole plan of action to Mr. Krishnan and Mr. Pillai. They too agreed that the plan seemed convincing enough and did make couple of changes. Before the project presentation and demos they would meet and also introduce the customer to the Managing Director and share some of the strategic investment plans that the company is doing for the project as well as practice. Chandran and I did feel that it would set a positive mood in the customer's mind and agreed to it.

25th Mar 2002

While we were getting ready, Chandran's phone was ringing and yes it was. Mr.Galasso informed that he was near Tidel Park. For all customer visits, we had a standard procedure of welcoming them and indeed the corporate services manager Mr. KK and Vijay were experts in this. They had put one office boy at the entrance with a placard and all security procedures were handled neatly. Mr.Galasso was at the ground floor in no time. Chandran went to the ground floor to receive and in the third floor, we gave him a grand welcome with garlands, pottu, bouquet and coconut water. We took him inside the conference room. Mr. Krishnan and Mr. Pillai also came to the conference room. I started the presentation with the agenda of what we would do over the next two days etc. Post my introductory presentation, Chandran pitched in to provide an update on how the POC progress is being made. I knew for sure was expecting a grand demo of the POC. All of us were trembling as to how Mr. Galasso would react. Not sure whether it was Dharani's hand or tumbler but could see his tumbler shaking. Raj, Subbarayulu and Lamech were profusely sweating. To my surprise Mr. Pillai and Mr. Krishnan were smiling and discussing possibly about the morning traffic woes while on their way to office. Probably, that is how senior management would keep themselves cool and light in potentially adverse situations. The first slide was POC status and Chandran had painted in red and without mincing words he told it is not yet done. I was keenly observing. Mr.Galasso's eyebrows were shaping sharp in anger. He was intensely looking at Chandran trying to seek answers as to why this wasn't told earlier and I could sense Chandran losing confidence. I quickly interrupted and boldly told "Galasso, the POC approach itself is incorrect." Mr. Galasso retaliated and told "I didn't plan this" for which I quoted the architecture document and IBM's confirmation note based on which the approach was finalized. However, I told, "there seems to be a problem at the protocol layer which lead to the current problem." Since I was the architect, Mr. Galasso was convinced partially. Chandran interrupted saying "Galasso, don't worry. We have some good news for you," and requested AK to demo the e-booth module. After that Chandran requested Raj to demo the search module and then the product catalogue was demoed by Subbarayulu and pricing and billing concepts were also showcased. Raj, Lamech and Subbarayulu were not only excellent technically but they were also great communicators. Also, they would know how to present to customers and convince them. One important aspect that I saw in all of them was the way they would handle a technical problem in calm manner. Possibly, this strength of them helped us pull the show in our favour.

I could sense a great relief in Mr. Galasso's eyes. He went on to ask "Why did you guys tell nothing is working?" Chandran interrupted and told that what he meant was the working of the end to end process. By this time, lunch was served and Chandran and I were greatly relieved.

Both of us were standing like left and right to and were keeping him occupied. We soon realized that we should allow him to talk to Mr. Krishnan and Mr. Pillai and in fact, that did help I would say. To our surprise, Mr. Krishnan was talking about Italian economics and Mr. Pillai on politics. Somehow time passed by and immediately post lunch we had scheduled for Mr. Krishnan's presentation.

Mr. Krishan's slides weren't any jazzy but very meaty and important. One of the critical promises he made was investing in training on epicentric and autonomy products and also hiring epicentric expert's time. Mr. Galasso quickly connected the dots and told this would help in ironing out technical problems and he sincerely appreciated Mr. Krishnan. He also suggested hiring IBM websphere consultant for which Mr. Krishnan gave approval immediately. Both Chandran and I were very excited with the turn of events. After a couple more sessions we took a day break and invited for a short evening tour. After Chandran and Galasso left I was seriously contemplating about the POC failure part and how to overcome the current situation. Soon Pillai came to my seat and called me to his cabin. Both of us were discussing about the day and the plus and minus of the various sessions delivered to . I told Mr. Pillai that though both of us felt good about the outcome, I was concerned about the POC failure part. Mr. Pillai explained that "Not all trivial/ obvious decisions are taken on day one". He also adviced about how I cannot own other's problems and failures on to myself and get bogged down in a corporate world. After some serious discussions I started feeling better and started enjoying as to how we managed the situation and how it contributed to the success for the whole team.

8

T-M-C
(Training-Mentoring-Coaching)

Post the decisions on investments on product training, I started exploring the possible training options. In a fixed price engagement, unless cost provisions are made during the proposals stage it is difficult to get approvals for investments. Even then both Krishnan and Pillai had indicated that only a "reasonable" amount can be spent. As the saying goes, "Innovation happens out of need", I thought I should do something different so that my overall training needs for the project is taken care till the end of the duration. So I had few options to consider,

a. Send someone senior to USA and get him trained on the product

b. Get a trainer from the USA and get the team trained

In option a), the risk is on the individual, for example if he quits the company or he falls sick or if he is unable to understand completely. Dependency on one individual becomes extremely high so I ruled out this option completely.

In option b), the training cost goes high as I have to take care of the trainers' accommodation etc. More importantly, I didn't have a large team to participate in the training program (Will explain the recruitment lessons separately in the coming chapters).

3rd Apr 2002

After multiple discussions with vendors and managers over the next two weeks, we formulated the following strategy,

a. Formed a three member core team for epicentric and autonomy products

b. Bought

   i. Online (Self learning courses)

   ii. Trainer provided (Audio mode-Regular theory classes

   iii. In India (Introductory, Architecture, Big picture, project, and Clarification)

We made AK the team lead for Epicentric Technology and Raj the team lead for autonomy and associated two developers each to AK and Raj. Simultaneously, we initiated recruitment for additional team members. In about two weeks the three member core team became fully aware of the product. By then we managed to recruit an additional six developers. On the third week we had the trainer provide the session and also made AK/Raj to take parallel sessions to new members. By the end of the third week, the core team was completely familiar with the product and other six members were aware of the product at a high level. During this week we also managed to establish a good connection with the trainer. Also, out of the six new members, we rejected two members and retained only four members who we felt were competent. We also shared our project requirements and requested to have a one-on-one "coaching" tailor-made based on our project needs.

In short, we structured the training program as "T-M-C" (Training-Mentoring-Coaching)

Training – Self-Learning / Online webinar

Mentoring- Audio/trainer

Coaching-in-person /trainer/Chennai

The beauty and success of this program structure was that we spent less than "one person–ten days- US trained" program and got ten people trained and also tailored to actually deliver specifically as per the project needs.

Also the critical success factor was the mentoring module which was built on top of the project requirement. This aspect helped us uncover the technical difficulties. Along with "T-M-C", we also included another twenty hours worth of online "email / chat" discussions that will help uncover further more project related doubts. This we actually utilized effectively on a regular basis. We used the same model for the rest of the products trainings too.

9

ESTIMATION

Critical success factor for every project is having the right people and in adequate numbers. Most of the project failures stem from this core aspect. Having said that, where does this problem start? This has been my concern from the beginning. Based on my earlier experiences and also based on my current analysis, I felt the reasons might be the ones listed below,

Right People- At the time of presale cycle

- Firstly understanding the project requirement is done by someone who is not qualified enough for the job. The reasons for this could be galore. Like the pace in which the technology changes, it is next to impossible for companies to hire or / create experts. Hence most of the time, we are all pushed to "manage". This is where the core problems start. Though ten to twenty percent buffer is apportioned most of the times it doesn't help.

  Secondly, during the elaboration phase the customer requirements go through significant changes due to which the estimates change too. Since expertise levels are slow with the people who are involved in the project, they are confident enough to fight it out with the customers and at the same time, the customer is also unwilling to accept for changes in effort.

Not having the right people at the start of the engagement has made an impact

   i.   In providing incorrect or lower efforts

   ii.   Accepting to deliver the requirements without analysing the solution for the problem.

To summarize, people with inadequate skills on the subject matter,

   a.   Quote incorrectly or low.

   b.   Accept to deliver impossible or difficult requirements using technology.

Though I have known all these, may be to some extent, at that time I was feeling helpless as I can't do much about what had already happened. I was not part of presale and initial phases of the project. However I definitely felt that I can't ignore the fact that the original estimates are in no way matching the current situations and decided to take it head on with customers and senior management.

I formed a small core team who would help me in analysing the gap/incorrectness in the estimates. In about a week we realized that this gap is too huge. After multiple initial discussions we presented the problem on hand to Mr. Pillai and Mr. Krishnan.

The initial reaction from them was "shocking". Yeah, we did expect it. However, we felt that it was better late than never. Mr. Pillai and Mr. Krishnan weren't convinced and asked all of us to prepare different kinds of report and data. After a couple of days of careful digging, analysis, discussions and deliberations, we created a huge PowerPoint deck and went and presented our findings to Mr. Pillai and Mr. Krishnan. By the end of the meeting, both of them realized that the problem is genuine and needed to be handled. They decided to take it up with the sales manager.

That evening was one of the best evenings during those project days. I was really relieved. I felt now, if the efforts are increased, something can be done to improve the project performance. Many of my colleagues also gave us confidence that once Mr. Krishnan and Mr. Pillai agree to take up any issue, they would somehow make it happen. With mixed feelings, I called it a day, college packed up my bags and started walking out. On my way back, I saw my senior college, Raghu holding filter coffee in his right hand and a Kings cigarette in his left hand. He was quite surprised to see me in Tidel Park as he thought I had gone to Singapore. After a quick recap I started talking about the project and the difficulties I am facing especially on the people's side. Raghu greatly appreciated the training (T-M-C) model. In fact, he told he would adopt this model (When I happened to see him few years later he was excitingly appreciating the success and relevancy of (T-M-C) model.)However, he raised a genuine question as to how I would be able to recruit another forty resources immediately and he told how much he is struggling to source good profiles. This is when it struck me hard that even if Mr. Krishnan and Mr. Pillai approves to the effort and hiring how am I going to recruit so many in so less time. With confused thoughts (evening happiness eroding) I reached home and called up Mr. Pillai and shared my concern. Mr. Pillai is generally well versed in handling these type of concerns. But now he too told he shares the same concern. Not knowing what to do, I slowly retired into the sofa and started watching TV. Doremon was playing and my daughter was seriously watching it. Seeing me, she immediately switched off the TV and both of us started playing with each other. Devi had cooked fried rice and brinjal salna (guess some special day.) Generally after a heavy dinner, both Devi and I go out for a small walk and we stepped out. Near our home, there is a "Sivan" temple and opposite to it "Ambica Appalam" store. This shop use to sell good snack items and thought it would be good idea to walk till Ambica store and eat paani puri. We got there and were sitting outside on the chairs. A big 21"TV (those days 21" itself was big) was playing Vijay TV. The title itself was very catching and in the program a sadhu was explaining how we should handle life problems "differently (maathiyosi)". This kind of struck hard and I was having my very own Eureka moment. Though it is a simple thought, I have always realized that a different approach solves lot of real life problems. I felt I should have the same approach for my recruitment problem.

10

RECRUITMENT

Typically in large corporates there is a dedicated recruitment team. They also use external vendors to support them in their recruitment activities. Roughly it takes about 8–12 weeks from sourcing - on boarding a candidate. I had a need of thirty resources and for that at least 300 resumes had to be sourced and it would roughly take about three weeks. All this put together the estimated time was roughly sixteen weeks which is four months and as per our project plan my UAT started in October which was roughly six months from then.

The other approach that I had was to recruit on "contract" model, hiring people who are on the vendor company's payroll. While this model will help in bringing down the fulfilment time, it came out with a different set of problems like

    a.   Quality of the resources could be relatively poor

    b.   The probability of they leaving the project without proper notice is very high

    c.   You cannot handover confidential modules to these resources

    d.   Payment to be made from day one of on boarding

I kind of felt both approaches to recruitment came with unique sets of problems.

11th Apr 2002

With all these confused thoughts, I was walking past Marie Curie hall for a quick coffee. It is like a 50 meter corridor walk and there are three big halls. Each one can seat around 200 people. In the third hall you have the HR team. The HR who hired me was Meera Nair. She had completed her MBA from a reputed school and she had a very unique talent of remembering the employee ID of every employee who joined the company. She was young, brilliant, beautiful, very helpful and supportive too. I was thinking about approaching Miss Meera and taking her inputs. Still engrossed in my thoughts, I ordered a "Ginger–Chukka" coffee. This was a popular item in that shop. To my surprise, Meera just came to coffee shop and both of us started exchanging stories. It looked like she heard a lot about my performance and she was advising to keep up the good work. After a short while, I explained my current problem and explained the need for thirty resources ASAP, and I also explained the solutions I was contemplating. Meera suggested that I should follow a hybrid approach

1. Do permanent hire and look for quick joinees and you can also consider giving joining bonus and you can also buy notice period.

2. Do contract–to–hire–model and not just contract model and advised as below.

   a. Provide job guarantee to the contract candidates on good performance.

   b. Structure the selection process as "two week-on the job work" model. If the candidate performs well then continue with the contract else discontinue.

   c. Engage with 2–3 vendors from whom you can get resources.

   d. Look at the problem solving capabilities and attitude towards work of the candidate and not just the technical know-how during the two weeks assessment.

I just followed what Meera advised. In a month's time I managed to recruit fifteen people on contract–to hire model and another five people on permanent hire model and a month later managed to hire another twenty resources. Out of the thirty resources (Ten buffer on contract side) we hired twenty resources in around 1. 5 months itself and the rest we hired after two months.

"Most of the people whom I recruited as contract resources whose English language skills and communications skills were below average are working as VP's and Directors in MNC's and large Indian IT organizations managing 100's and thousands of people and have settled as US citizens... The critical success factor of hiring is to look at the attitude of the person and not just syntax knowledge. Another critical factor while interviewing is to test what the resource knows and not what the interviewee knows."

II

STRUCTURE

It was a nice Sunday evening, Devi and Kansi (my daughter) had gone to visit my in-laws' house. This kind of gave me ample free time and just strolled out for a break and got into "Durga Bhavan". This restaurant has been in existence for more than three decades and remained in the same corner of the main road. The speciality of the restaurant is the quality of the food and the consistency in taste and the menu items. Also the menu items were limited in numbers which made it slightly easy to choose from the menu. On Sundays, the special is "adai and keeraivadai". Along with this "bonda" and "vazakkai bajji" served with white chutney (coconut based) and sambar is equally in demand all days. So regular customers kind of knew what to expect and what to eat on a particular day and time. I ordered keerai vadai and a plate of bonda. Keeraivadai takes a bit of longer duration to serve and while sitting freely I was observing the environment. Around ten tables were placed and roughly forty people would be dining and roughly ten people were waiting in queue for someone to finish eating and clear the table. Along with the customers, there were around ten people who were serving food, taking orders, billing and collecting money. The interesting part about these people was their "age". None of them were of same age group. The people who were serving were young and old. Order takers were middle aged, supervisors were old, billers were middle aged and packers young etc. Also, another interesting part was no one was reporting to anyone including the supervisor. All of them were doing their jobs on their own with minimal supervision. The supervisor actually understood that supervision was done for the customers and not for the workers. In our industry the "pyramid" structure is kind of forced. The roles created were also to manage people and not the work. Like for example, team lead-one who leads team of members, project lead –leads team leaders and project manager – lead's project leaders. In this model, people are only managing people (their needs, wants, aspiration, likes, dislikes etc.) and effectively only the team members "work" and rest of them effectively "extracting work" from one another. Over a period of time the "leads" just know to "manage" people "and "extract work" and "manage situations" and "handle escalations". At this junction, they kind of loose their respect of the team members and their ability to extract work effectively goes down. And now in order to prove their supremacy with their team, politics comes into picture and politics is the birth of project failure.

I had completely forgotten my keerai vadai while I got engrossed into the structure thinking. My keeraivadai with kara chutney arrived. My bonda with white chutney also arrived. Now I was kind of thinking why different chutneys for keerai vadai and bonda and that made me feel that when eating together the dishes have to compliment each other and not compete with each other. Likewise, the hotel employees roles were also complimenting and they were neither "competing" nor just "extracting work".

These thoughts were going deep into my mind and drawing parallels with my project scenario. By this time, most of the recruitment as per revised estimations, training, requirements gathering and proof of technical concepts all were done and we were missing detailed design and coding phase of the project. And this is the time I felt the team should be formed with appropriate structure.

Definitely, I was against the regular pyramid and supervisor structure that prevailed in our industry. I deeply believed that in knowledge industry, supervision is absolutely not required and especially supervision to make things "faster" is ridiculous. I felt I should adopt the Durga Bhavan structure with the below rules followed,

a. Roles should be complimentary

b. No or minimal people supervision

c. Age / Designation doesn't matter

d. Sub Teams to be created based on customer delivery modules

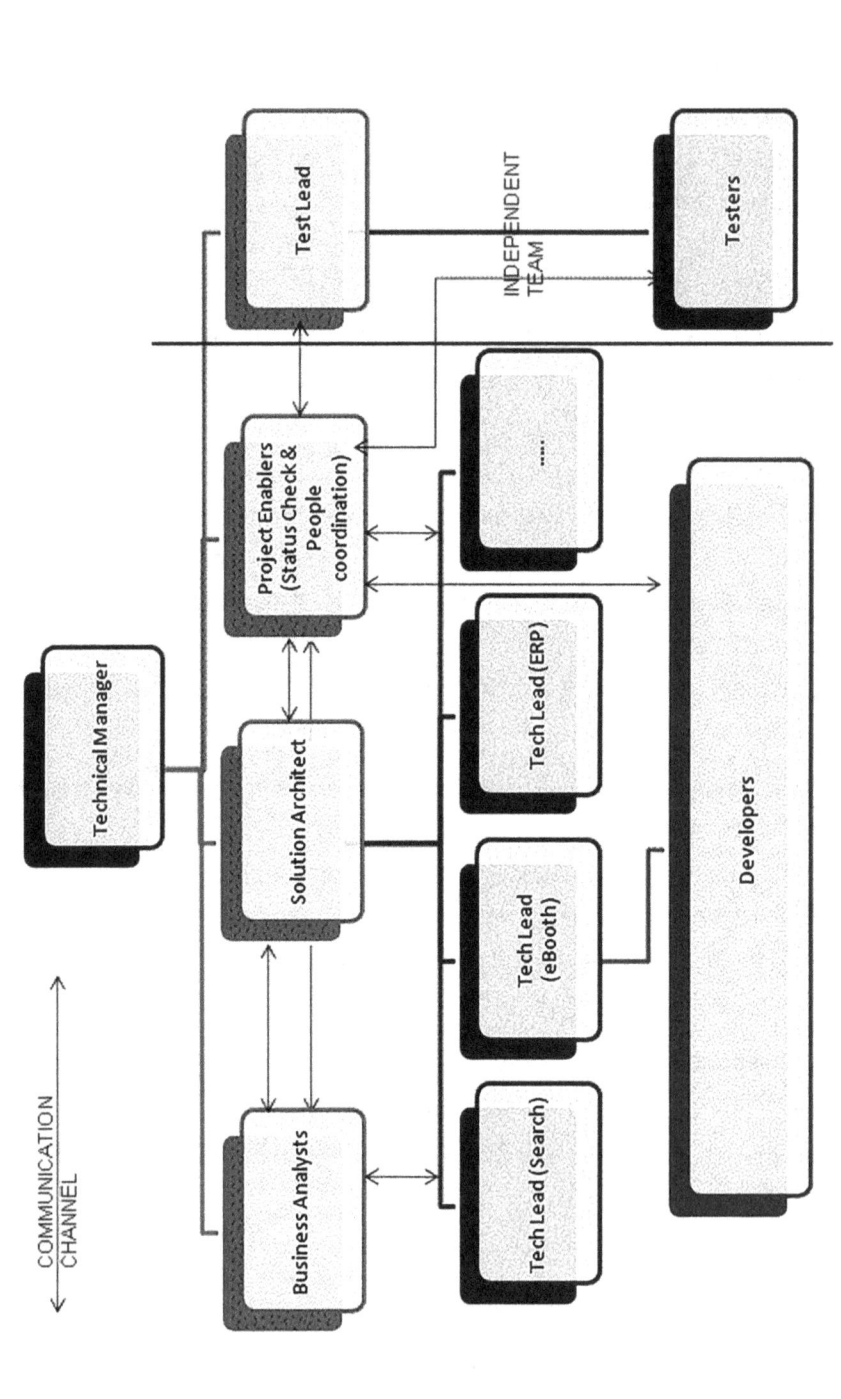

12

WALK AROUND

6th May 2002

It was almost 6:50PM when I came out of Mr. Krishnan's room. Obviously my face had gone pale. What else could be the reason except for status meeting (Normally both Mr. Krishnan and Mr. Pillai support us during customer escalation calls). Yeah, though they did agree and encourage to the fact that a lot of progress has been made, they told that we were far behind the final milestone. At this time, I almost had a sixty member team (when I started it was just an eight member team) got them trained on the products, had collected the requirements from the customer to a large extent. But still, the progress hasn't been satisfactory is how I would see myself and that is exactly what both Mr. Krishnan and Mr. Pillai advised too.

During the meeting, Mr. Krishnan said "Mega you have a good handle on the project in terms of "what the problem is", "where the problem is", "who the problem is," but probably what is missing is "why" and 'how' you or your team is going to resolve. While I was trying to understand and defend that 'why' is a technical problem and too much of my involvement as project manager will create issues with the technical architects, Mr. Pillai quickly intervened and shared that 'why' needn't be technical alone and many a times it could be "non-technical" only. Though I accepted his views, I wasn't sure how to unearth "not to be seen-non technical" problem.

While I was breaking my head, I had a strong push on my shoulder and with a jerk I looked back and it was Kasinath. Kasinath is the senior most person in our team and the most diligent and smart Business Analyst. The customer himself wouldn't argue with him as he would have all the minute details and it will be 100% correct. Looking at my face Kasinath immediately reacted and asked me why am I dull. After listening to me, he offered coffee at the ground floor of Tidel Park. While coming in the elevator, Kasinath, in a crystal clear tone told, "Mega you have done the best job so far as a project manager. In less than eight weeks, you built a 50+ members team, got the training done, put together a clear deliverable based structure. Everything is perfect but that doesn't mean having all these will ensure success on its own." I fully agreed with what Kasinath described but still the problem remained unsolved. How to "quickly" and "exactly" or "correctly" identify and understand the root cause of the problem. As mentioned earlier, employing people in supervisory role isn't going to help us. The developers are currently very productive, motivated and working hard. Also I don't believe in that role at all and I wasn't in for it too. Kasinath intersected my chain of thoughts and told "Just walk around Mega and engage in casual and professional conversation with all the team members twice a day. This informal one-to-one conversation in/near the team members' seat will uncover lots of problems which could be a deterrent to the project's progress. Also while walking around the team members' bay you need not sit in everyone's place but just move on and sit only in those who you really feel they are in some serious trouble. The essence here is "casual conversation". Right now, in your structure there isn't enough "people management" happening. The tech leads are doing design and code review and your solution architect is problem solving. So possibly some of the "people nuances" aren't coming out quickly and freely." I kind of felt that Kasinath had made a solid point. From the next day onwards I started "walking around" and had "casual conversations".

Yes, indeed it did work. When I was talking to Rajesh, epicenteric portal developer, working on e-booth module he opened up on how his "product problem" is belittled and questioned by the solution architect and which is becoming a deter to many of his tasks. And on the next day, Deepa was mentioning about her parents initiative on match making and her disinterest etc. The first walk around went for about an hour and I could sense that I learnt more than during the regular status meetings.

13

FIRE IN THE BELLY

3rd June 2012

Further to the adoption of "walk around" and "casual conversation" we did see a lot of improvement in lot of areas and it did increase overall team productivity. But still that wasn't sufficient for us to deliver on time. The amount of pending deliverables vs. available time was always high. All of us including the customer know that we are all putting our genuine efforts and all of us were of the opinion that we can't do much anymore. But somehow myself and Mr. Galasso was hell bent on launching the online trade fair portal before the year end. I decided that while "walking around", I will try and observe even more details. But somehow I couldn't really recognize.

It was a Friday evening and while I was trying to decipher the problem I saw that almost all of them had left for the day and myself, Chandran and AK were the only three left in the whole of Curie hall. I too felt like calling it a day and all three of us left together. Next day morning I woke up early as I didn't get a lot of sleep. In the morning Devi was asking me why I was disturbed and I told her the various initiatives in recruitment, training, "walk around" and "casual conversation" concepts but still how we are lagging and my interest to launch the portal for the year end. Devi was also losing out on ideas and finally the discussion topics rested on "exam time" and how she used to study the entire book in two weeks and score distinction. Suddenly this struck me hard. I thought that the next six months, July-December I should make it like two levels of exams. As a coincidence our first UAT was scheduled on 1st Oct and BETA launch on Christmas day. So I thought that the1stof October could be like a board exam date. Thanking Devi for giving a wonderful idea and feeling relieved, I started getting ready for office. It was around 10:30AM when I entered the third floor Nancy was like "Enna sir first day challenge a?" I smiled back and she heartily said that "Sir you are putting a lot of effort and I am sure you will win it". Though I felt happy I retaliated and told it's not just me but my entire team is working hard. She quickly told that "Sir I won't agree completely. May be you, Chandran, AK, Raj, Lamech, Subbarayulu and few others maybe working hard but not the rest sir. Even now when you get into Curie hall you will be the first person and probably the only person." As she told, I was the only person and in half an hour's time Mr. Krishnan walked past me. Seeing me he turned back and started chatting casually. Mr. Krishnan is generally a man of few words but actually that day he seemed opposite. He was talking about many random subjects and the discussion kind of settled on Expoworld project. Mr. Krishnan appreciated the significant improvements in various areas including customer satisfaction. However, he also mentioned that the go live dates are approaching and he is observing that we are lagging. Mr. Krishnan did acknowledge that the team is working hard. However he pointed out that not everyone are working hard as some of us and not with the same passion. He went on to say that the below points should be followed

a. Sense of urgency

b. Passion to deliver and succeed

c. Working hard

Not just one or few team members but by all. He also advised that as a leader I should bring in those above points into every one's mind and soul. After Mr. Krishnan left my cubicle I started feeling on "exam date", "sense of urgency" and "passion to deliver" and "working hard".

Net-net, after deeper analysis I felt that all or most of us were "hardworking" and "highly passionate" too but what was probably missing was the sense of urgency. I was kind of thinking what Devi was telling about the "exam" concept. While I was writing it down, Chandran too came to the office along with Raj and Lamech and Subbaryulu and when we all decided to go to Tidel coffee shop AK and Kums also joined us. Kumaran (kums as we call him) is a silent achiever and always smiling. He would dissipate many of my tensions and make me feel how easy everything would be done. After reaching downstairs, Chandran was asking about my concerns and I started explaining the discussions that I had with Devi and Mr. Krishnan and my analysis and viewpoints. Chandran and all readily agreed with my analysis. We started discussing about how we can bring in the "sense of urgency".

Until now all of us were chasing the Beta Go live date (25-12-2002), which is six months away. We all quickly decided that we should target "UAT" date and not the go live date. UAT was on 1st-Oct-2002 (01-10-02)and we bought ten colour charts and wrote 01-10-02 in big fonts covering the whole chart and stuck in all the places within Curie hall. We did not write anything else in the chart but just the plain date using red colour sketch pen on yellow colour chart paper. More than half of the Curie hall was seated by Expoworld team. Not just limiting to Curie hall we also stuck the chart paper in the reception area and in the corridor area.

After instructing corporate services team to take care of the chart papers, we all went back to our homes with loads of satisfaction, happiness and also anxiety as we weren't sure whether this will work.

Monday morning around 11:00AM my team slowly started coming up to me asking if I knew anything about (01-10-02). Interestingly, the numbers were a bit unique in the sense it was made up of 0, 1 and 2. Slowly by the end of the day, the entire Curie hall was talking about the numbers and the chart. In the meanwhile, Mr. Pillai sent an email to the entire floor team and asked people to tell their ideas, and also announced that the lucky person would be rewarded too. To our great surprise, two people from our team had written back correctly and sent an email to Mr. Pillai. The next day morning Mr. Pillai called for a floor meeting and gave away a parker pen to the two lucky team members and he also gave a pep-talk on the importance of the UAT date. I still feel that this pep-talk by Mr. Pillai was an essential turning point towards the project success. By the end of the floor meeting we could sense that 01-10-02 was getting its required importance and attention in the teams' mind.

Yes, the needed "fire-in-the-belly" has been created and the "sense of urgency" has also been created in every one's mind to a large extent.

14

GLASS FILTERS

The entire team of 50+ people were working really hard chasing the 01-10-02 UAT goal. The bonding between myself and all the other team members seemed to be increasing a lot. In fact, we started realizing that some of the members got engaged, some got married and few had new babies in their families and couple of love stories in this team too. More or less we were becoming like one big family. We had regular group lunch sessions and we used to go to a snack shop during night stays and buy bread omelette and watermelon or orange juice.

One day Chandran called me out for a coffee. When Chandran calls for "coffee" it means he is going to say something very serious. I couldn't think of any specific project related problems. With a confused mind I sat with him for coffee. Chandran went blunt on me and said "Mega why are you always harsh and unreasonable on Mani and Prabhu". He went on to say that more or less I am ill-treating or treating in a step-motherly way. Hearing this from Chandran, I became quite upset and was speechless for sometime. Seeing my reaction Chandran was a bit shocked. Chandran then tried to pacify me and asked me to take this in a positive stride. After a while I was back to my normal self. Chandran's feedback was hurting me. I wasn't upset with Chandran but the very statement that Mani and Prabhu got step-motherly treatment did hurt me deep. I was quietly sitting in my cubicle and thinking deeply. Mr. Pillai passed by my cubicle and seeing me upset he started talking to me. Slowly I opened up and shared the feedback from Chandran. Mr. Pillai nodded his head and told me some interesting facts

- Myself, Chandran, AK, Raj, Lamech, Subbarayulu, Mani and Prabhu were in the team together from the very beginning of the project. There has been times when both Chandran and I had raised concerns about Mani and Prabhu's performance.

- Now Chandran thinks Mani and Prabhu are doing well but I continue to bash them.

- I felt what Mr. Pillai said was correct but wasn't sure about the reasons.

Mr. Pillai then explained the concept of "glass filters". These filters are the opinions and views or biases that we form about an individual over a period of time based on their behaviour, work style, attitude etc. Over a period of time, these opinions strongly etch into our minds and creates a filter in front of our eyes. Later whenever we interact with the person we end up seeing the person through the filters and not just the problem. So we don't deal with the problem as "problem" but "Mani problem" or "Prabhu problem". Mr. Pillai went on to say that possibly I am carrying a biased opinion about Mani and Prabhu which is why a simple and regular problem sounds like a complex one and unsolvable. I felt this as logical and quite possible and over the next few days I was observing myself and my conversations with Mani and Prabhu and the way I deal with them and their problems. I started realizing what Mr. Pillai told and felt how startling the truth was.

15

IMPERFECT IS PERFECT

15th Sep 2002

After the 01-10-02 initiative, things started moving in a much faster pace. We were almost ready with all the development work but we were sure it had enough bugs and it was not fully integrated too. At the same time, we also had to setup an environment at client location (Italy). The entire environment had been setup by the customer including development, test, and production. Much of all of these tasks we had made sure that the customer completed. We were in the middle of September and only two more weeks for UAT. We had two choices

1. To postpone the UAT date
2. Initiate the UAT with bugs

First option is an easy choice. We may have to face the beatings from customers and senior management but you will get more time. However, it doesn't guarantee that UAT would be smoother either and also whether the additional time would be sufficient for us to deliver.

The second option was to initiate the UAT with bugs (known defects). Though this model will expose you to the customer, there are lots of advantages like

a. You get to deploy your code in customer testing environment.
b. You get to test your application during "cut" phase which will minimize the number of "changes" during the actual "UAT" phase.

c. The customer involvement, almost six weeks early, brought in a whole new perspective to the project delivery (flip side is if you don't have full control over the customer and/or if the customer isn't cooperative or favourable this model will back fire).

d. Since the defects were coming straight from the customer, the mental compulsion to fix the defects quicker and faster for the team members was very high.

Weighing all these, we approached the customer to deliver the application with known bugs. The customer was originally hesitant but based on our commitments he agreed for the second option.

Including the customer we all knew it was easier said than done. Performing UAT means a lot to the customer's management stakeholders. At the minimum they have to spend on hiring people who will do the user testing and who would become their users too subsequently. Deploying code with known bugs sounds like a nice term but at the core the very first day the trust on our delivery would be lost. After losing that trust it may be next to impossible to bring it back. So while "imperfect is perfect" model sounds strategic what is critical is how the whole strategy gets implemented.

It was Monday morning and we were all fresh after a hectic week and restful Sunday. The Sunday rest was the most needed for all of us. Categorically we all decided we wouldn't disturb each other on the Sunday's and take good rest. This policy had helped us to work long hours for months together without much fatigue in the mind and body. Chandran, AK, Raj, Lamech, Kums and Subbarayulu and I got into Newton conference room for discussing on our strategy to handle the most bold decision that we all took. We were actually surprised that the customer too agreed for it. While we were in serious discussions, Mr. Pillai stepped into the Newton room. Contrary to his regular style, Mr. Pillai, was quiet and observant. The biggest strength of Mr. Pillai and Mr. Krishnan was the ability to provide complete freedom and at the same time having complete control on the engagement. Though this was a big decision, we as a team decided to go ahead with this decision. Over the week end during my casual chats with Mr. Pillai I had told about this bold decision. Initially he was reluctant but then he didn't wanted to interfere or discourage and hence probably did not disagree to it I guess. Hence, when Mr. Pillai saw the project leadership team sitting inside the Newton room (this room is on the way to Mr. Pillai's cabin) he wished to understand the decision little deeper. After a little while and hearing to our conversations, Mr. Pillai requested to interfere and share his views. We were actually pleased and immediately agreed to it. Mr. Pillai firstly appreciated the bold decision and expressed his surprises as how the customer agreed to do this and went on to say that "this actually means that the customer has lots of trust in all of you guys and that is the exact reason why he had agreed to do this. Performing UAT with known bugs means a lot of rework for the customer team. After a short pause, Mr. Pillai started talking again. Mr. Pillai has a knack of articulating without using jargons but through simple examples. He went on to explain, "In any critical problem situation, people don't think about why or who created the problem but what they all care is how well the problem or situation is handled. Now the critical situation is,

1. Our ability to launch the project by end of this year

2. Our ability to manage the customer expectations created due to testing an application with full of bugs. He further explained that it is important we quickly fix the defects and in parallel work on stabilizing the application and not just get bogged down with the UAT defects on hand.

All of us felt confident about our decision and moved on performing UAT without knowing how each of our personal lives are going to be completely affected due to the heavy work.

16

NIGHT WATCHMAN

6th Oct 2002

It was Sunday around 01:00PM and many of us were in office trying to fix the bugs. At times many of our team members were cursing our decision about why we agreed to perform UAT on an application that wasn't even properly unit tested. Since early June, the entire team was stretching a lot spending more than 12 hours every day but somehow we managed to not let the fatigue creep into them. We had held the spirits high. However, we started feeling that the team was feeling discouraged. Chandran, AK, Raj, Kums, Lamech and Subbarayulu got together and decided that we will stop getting worried about the application bugs and focus on motivating the team as we all knew that we have to travel another three months for actual application launch. We decided we will go out for a late lunch and probably go to the beach and play and just relax. We stepped out around 2PM and went to a nice beach side multi cuisine restaurant in ECR road and we were only eating till around 4:00PM. After almost heavy lunch some of us strolled out to the shores and we were walking relaxed. Girls continued their chatting inside and some boys started playing cricket inside the resort shade. While walking we could sense how much relieved the entire team were. We felt we did the right thing by breaking the bug fixing routine and we consciously decided we will not discuss anything about the project with the team today. At the same time we were equally worried as how we can keep the team motivated to perform over the next 3–4 months but consciously decided we too will break from the project discussions for today. Probably the leadership team was also getting fatigue. While everyone were chilling out and relaxing, my mind was continuously racing to fix this problem. After a short while I just skipped out and sat on the shore and observing blue waves. It was interesting to see that the waves were looking mild while it was far and when it reaches the shore the waves were wild and roaring and threatening you. However, immediately the waves retreats back into the sea as if it got frightened seeing you stare at them but only to come back with even more wilder. Suddenly, I sensed that the waves were really getting wilder than before and quickly got up and ran farther. When I turned back and saw, the waves again retreated back into the sea but this time with laughter and smiles possibly. I felt ashamed that I dared not the waves by sitting there. I remembered the phrase that Mr. Shankar (another boss of mine) always told me, "alai oindhu thalai muzuginatha saritharamillai" meaning "one can never take bath in sea if he waits for the waves to stop". Mr. Shankar always advocates "that one has to face problems and solve it and not run away. When you run away the problems laugh at you and when you face it you laugh at the problems." While I was engrossed in my thinking Lamech and Subbarayulu came to me asking me to join the cricket match. I too felt that I should go join the team and rest the problems for a while.

Like the waves in the beach the first email I noticed in my mail box the next day morning was from Mr. Galasso asking when we will close the 200+ bugs that got opened up in the last one week. Seeing the email I was upset and saddened. I was the only guy sitting in my cubicle. Since we took a break the previous day (ha haha... I know you are thinking it was a Sunday and it was supposed to be a holiday) no one had turned up to the office on time. I was staring at the email without knowing what to do. Slowly I could sense that we were in a web of problems and it is important I attack all of them in parallel and not in silos. I thought it would be prudent to first categorise them and started penning the details.

- Customer side
  - Firstly lower the expectations in terms of the speed in which we will fix the problem and the number of problems that will be fixed etc.
  - Increase the knowledge levels of the customer team who are testing the application. Though Mr. Galasso knows 100% of the requirements, his team (hired all them very recently) wasn't aware of the application and its functionalities to a large extent.

- o Make Chandran travel to Italy and be involved at onsite to handle the customer expectations as well as conduct series of workshops to its users and make them understand the application fully.
- Defects
  - o Classify the defects as "look and feel", "functional" and "show stoppers".
  - o Further classify the "functional" defects as "low/medium/complex" and accordingly prioritize the defects.
  - o Chandran and Mr. Galasso would decide the defect type and their priority levels and the technical teams would fix them based on the allocated priority.
- Team
  - o Core team should be formed onsite (Italy) who will be involved in fixing the "show stoppers" quickly and fix certain "functional" defects.
  - o Core team to be formed at offshore who will focus on controlling the environment, source code and work on "complex" functional defects and who will focus on stabilizing the application.
  - o Everyone of us to put additional efforts similar to running fast at the end of the marathon race. I decided that I will lead the team from the front and run faster than before.
- Environment
  - o The customer side environment will be the testing environment and the teams will have access to it.
  - o Will have separate development and test environments and will make incremental changes to the development environment.

As our response to customer's defect fixing email, Chandran and I had long discussions with the customer and highlighted our plans. Mr. Galasso was welcoming all the moves and he too agreed to all the changes that we intended to make.

Within a week we initiated every decision. Chandran, AK, Raj, Lamech and Subbarayulu all got their visas and tickets. Raj, Lamech and Subbarayulu left early to their homes for packing. AK mentioned he will leave a little later as his wife was packing for him. After a while Chandran also left and all of us got engrossed in our regular works. Suddenly I realized that AK still hasn't gone home and when I approached him he bluntly asked me not to disturb him. Then when I enquired the team they informed me that he was working on a "show stopper" problem and he was upset that his code was the cause for the "show stopper" problem. Generally AK is a soft person but at times I have seen him getting very upset and he wouldn't listen to anyone. I knew it was getting late for his flight and in another 8 hours he has to be at home but here he is fighting with a piece of code. Knowing AK well I decided not to disturb him and then called up his wife to check on the progress. To my shock she told that she hasn't done any packing as there was no proper big suitcase that can pack clothes for three months travel and when I further asked her what happened she remained quiet. She told that AK was supposed to come home with a suitcase a little early and then do all the packing. I was quiet for a while and then called her up and told I will take care of it. Then Devi and I went to T. Nagar Wipro bags shop purchased a big VIP suitcase and travelled in our Maruthi car to AK's house in Ambattur. It was a pretty long drive. After reaching home, Devi and AK's wife packed up the suitcase and all was kept ready. Around three hours later AK was rushing home fully tensed and when he saw us and everything packed he couldn't control himself and literally wept off. It took a little while for AK's wife to console him but at the end AK beamingly said to me that he had fixed the "show stopper" with all pride in his face. Seeing this AK's wife broke and started weeping and hugged him. Guess she was very angry that AK didn't pick up her phone calls but when she realized that we had travelled such a long distance to buy and bring the suitcase so that AK can continue with his last minute efforts and the way "strong" AK beamed with tears on the success of his work probably made her break down and understand the passion of the people who are working on this project or probably on a mission. Quickly we bid good bye and allowed them to spend the few hours before travel more happily.

The next few weeks and months we all were working hard. In fact I heard later that people used to call me the night watchman and there have been instances where people have stayed in office working nonstop for 60–70 hours without any force and compulsion. We guess it was just that passion which made us work like that probably.

17

MISSION IMPOSSIBLE

28th Dec 2002

It was a Saturday and most of us were relaxed actually. Yeah, we had made a beta launch as planned, of course with some bugs still on it (you know we are bold people by now.) and the customer was all pretty happy. The entire onsite team after a long continuous work had enjoyed the Christmas holiday. Mr.Galasso had arranged a big feast at his home to his entire team including Chandran, AK, Raj, Lamech and Subbarayulu. While I was just clearing my old emails, I heard a pop sound on my computer and saw an email with the subject as "congratulations". Yeah!!! I couldn't believe that Mr. Galasso had sent a congratulatory email terming the work that we did as "Mission Impossible". I read the email a few times. While I was still re-reading the email Mr. Krishnan was standing next to my cubicle and with all smiles he said "congrats Mega" this is indeed a big achievement. While I was thanking him my phone was ringing and yes it was from Mr. Pillai and he was also praising me. Probably the best moments of my life. Probably a sense of achievement. Quickly I shared this email and joy to the entire onsite and offshore teams and congratulated every one of our team members as without them, their passion and dedication this could not have been possible. After lots of congratulation emails and phone calls I was in no mood to work and thought I should call it a day and was actually feeling that I should dedicate this "Congratulatory Note" to Devi who stood by me throughout the year.

30th Dec 2002

It was around 11:00AM and I slowly entered the office. Nancy caught my attention and she started talking to me. Since it was already late I was in a hurry to step inside but she was refusing to cut the conversations. She was appreciating our success and when she realized that I am getting restless she subtly looked behind her on the wall. I was jumping in joy. Yeah you guessed it right. Nancy had taken the pain to put this testimony in the reception hall as the first thing in the morning. Seeing the testimony hanging on the wall, my mind travelled a year back and was recollecting Varun, the draconian, his atrocities and the personal challenge I took to myself. Once a star performer made into a nonperformer and now standing as a hero in front of Nancy, my team and the entire unit. Yeah, through this book I would like to request all our IT companies to bring in some prudent processes especially when they decide to fire people for whatsoever reasons. Be it performance or cost or no project or whatsoever be it. I heard couple of people, who were retrenched along with me, took/contemplated to take extreme steps as they found it difficult to get a job and also maintain their families and day-to-day lives. The companies probably wanted to eliminate low performers or reduce cost. Instead of building prudent processes that will uncover timely poor performances and help improve the performance of individuals, organizations wait till the end and when they realize the shareholders beat them down for their low profits companies quickly retort to these tactics and paint the picture of poor performance and retrench. While this practice may be prevalent in the developed nations, here we do not have social security in the case of job loss. These days the retrenchments are happening more to people who are playing the midlevel manager roles who are at the age of 40+. Typically these groups of people would have EMI commitments, children's education and social strata and when suddenly they are made to face this problem there is all possibility that they could take extreme steps. Also, the problem complicates as companies do not want to pay very high and take highly experienced people. Rather they are happy paying slightly more for a young manager who has more time and energy and passion.

Once again I would request the IT companies to be prudent while implementing retrenchments. Though I have slightly detracted, this is a very important social problem and more so considering the global industry dynamics that is happening presently.

Mega,
I want you to extend my personal congratulations and thank you to the entire offshore and onsite teams for having made Expoworld go live.

You (and us) have been assigned a task that could have been easily named "Mission Impossible" but, thanks to your skills, perseverance and hard work you have completed the mission successfully.

It costed a lot of days and nights in the office, sacrificing your personal life and interests. But now you can tell your families, friends and collegues, with whom you have not been in touch so frequently in the past weeks: "I was there and I made it happen!".

And you must be very proud for this achievement!

Now, like for every successful movie there is a second episode, we are ready to start "Mission impossible 2".
But I have no doubts that, since we have made it happen once, we will definitely make it a success again.

Thank you to all of you, and be ready for the next mission.

18
SUMMARY

Any big results happen because of the small steps taken. While the steps can be small it is important they be strategic in nature and that is the reason of my title "How to KISS (Keep It Simple and Strategic)?" Whatever I have tried to articulate are regular and simple things that happen in our day-to-day lives and which have been taught to us by our elders in simple terms except for few which are typical technical concepts.

Burning Desire – this trait is most important for any success. Hence as managers it is important he/she should have the burning desire to succeed and he/she should also imbibe this desire or goal in the minds of every team member.

Trust Self – from our childhood we would have been told about this but failure breeds when the manager doesn't carry this in his / her mind. Development projects are like building castles in air. It happens with lots of assumptions, constraints and limitations. If the manager has to win first he/she should believe that they can implement what the customer wants.

Big Picture– If development projects are like building castles in air, then unless everyone visualizes the castle it is next to impossible for the manager to deliver the project successfully.

Planning – starting our school days we have been preached about planning but still we continue to miss it. Only when you plan to a detailed level (8 hours / task) you will be able to unearth the possible limitations, constraints, shortcomings etc. the more limitations and constraints the more mitigations you can implement.

Complimentary skills – everyone respects everyone mainly because of the knowledge one possesses. Likewise the project manager should create structure that will complement each other and not compete.

Walk around – it may sound very simple but the truth of the matter is that it is the most profound strategy. This is when the project manager will become hands on and will solve real problems else project managers will be solving imaginary problems.

Glass filters – it is a philosophical concept and difficult to follow but if the project manager can follow this concept he will become a true leader who is empathetic and unbiased.

Imperfect is perfect – as a global village I believe this world is made up of imperfections and possibly surviving because of imperfections only. So project managers should know how to work around with constraints and convert constraints into solutions.

Face the problem – we keep hearing and studying in newspapers how young adults till elderly people commit suicide and the main reason is that they see the problem but unable to face it. Every small or big problem is solvable if we can handle it correctly. I wish and hope this book has satisfied your expectations.

WISH YOU ALL THE VERY BEST.

JAI HIND!!

19

GOOD LUCK

I sincerely hope that all these simple and yet strategic tips and words of wisdom would be useful to you and for the success of your project.

All the tips, however, is of no use if you don't put them into practice as is or after customising to your project requirement.

Remember that the joy is in innovation. Do dare and apply new and artistic concepts into your project and experience success. You will be thrilled at the outcomes.

20
DIGITAL RETREATS

Digital retreat is a 1 or 2 days getaway workshop conducted for aspiring or practicing "digital" projects managers to help succeed on their projects through artisistic project implementation techniques and not just limiting to the theoretical project management rules.

The Digital retreat takes place at a secluded farm house in the middle of a 4 acre farm in a beautiful little town, Tiruthani, in Tamilnadu. This retreat will offer a break from the daily distractions and also from the stress that the project problems may bring to you. This retreat also includes a spiritual and divine darshan of Lord Murugan at the hill top.

21

INVITE MEGAVARNAN AS A SPEAKER

Digital Architect, Business Strategist and Motivational speaker Megavarnan has presented many technical workshops to many of his fortune 500 customers across the globe.

Megavarnan has down-to-earth perspectives on project delivery and has successfully delivered very large digital programs to fortune 500 customers himself. Having successfully built a digital consulting firm as an entrepreneur, he is also a business author, and an acclaimed keynote speaker.

He presents inspiring concepts that will uncover the invisible and simplest problem causing major havocs in deep red projects. Through stories, anecdotes, practical jokes, some self-deprecation and even failure and pain, he shows how projects and businesses can overcome perceived limitations and set a higher bar for success and reach them.

Discover for yourself the benefits of artistic management styles in technical project management through his Digital Retreat workshops.

NOTES

HOW TO REACH
MEGAVARNAN

Email : gmegavarnan@gmail.com

Ph : +91- 8939605254

Facebook : https://www.facebook.com/megavarnan

Linked in : https://www.linkedin.com/in/megavarnan/